WHAT ANIMAL

WHAT ANIMAL

Poems by Oni Buchanan

The University of Georgia Press | Athens and London

Published by the University of Georgia Press

Athens, Georgia 30602

© 2003 by Oni Buchanan

All rights reserved

Designed by Mindy Basinger Hill

Set in 11/13.5 Fournier

Printed and bound by Thomson-Shore

The paper in this book meets the guidelines for
permanence and durability of the Committee on
Production Guidelines for Book Longevity of the
Council on Library Resources.

Printed in the United States of America

07   06   05   04   03   P   5   4   3   2   1

Library of Congress Cataloging-in-Publication Data

Buchanan, Oni, 1975–

What animal : poems / by Oni Buchanan.

p. cm.

ISBN 0-8203-2567-8 (pbk. : alk. paper)

I. Title.

PS3602.U33 W47 2003

811'.6—dc21

2003010598

British Library Cataloging-in-Publication Data available

*This book is dedicated
to my mother, Robin Welte, and
to my sister, Kelly Buchanan.*

Contents

Acknowledgments   ix
The Ducks and the Bicycle   xi

I.

Report from the Congregation of Invisibles   3
The Winter of the Primary Things   5
Tide Chart   6
Minutes from the Tuesday Meeting   8
The Only Yak in Batesville, Virginia   9
The Sheep Who Fastened the Sky to the Ground   10
Sweets to the Sweet   11
Mid-Afternoon   12
Synodic Month   13
Uncertainty Principle   14

II.

Reliquary   17
The Bearing   18
The Last Crwth Player   20
The Rescue Lullaby   21
The Guinea Pig and the Green Balloon   22
The Walk   24
The Large   25

III.

The Girls   29
Quota   30
Blood Weight   32
Cinch Song   34
The Term   35
Room 40   37
The Dusk Haruspicy   40

IV.

Night Shift   45
Cryptography   47
The Foist Grid   49
Queen Regent Queen Regnant   51
Hourglass   53
Transporter   55

V.

Dry   67
Rent   68
In the Third Hand   70
What Animal   72
Pastoral   74
Land Transaction on the Grass Swathe   76
Independence Day   78
Tercets for the End of Time   80

ACKNOWLEDGMENTS

I would like to thank the editors of the following journals and magazines in which some of the poems in this collection previously appeared: *American Letters & Commentary*, *Arts & Letters*, *Barrow Street*, *Black Warrior Review*, *can we have our ball back?*, *The Canary*, *Colorado Review*, *Conduit*, *Fence*, *Gulf Coast*, *Iowa Journal of Cultural Studies*, *Lit Magazine*, *Quarterly West*, *Seneca Review*, and *Verse*. Thank you to all of my instructors for their poetic guidance and encouragement. I am grateful to my peers at Iowa, University of Virginia, Harvard, Prague, Bucknell, and elsewhere, for their invaluable criticism and advice. I am also indebted to my students at Iowa for their tremendous inspiration. Finally, I could not have completed this project without the support of my family and my friends, all of whom it is my extraordinary blessing to know. And with deepest respect, thank you to Jon Woodward.

THE DUCKS AND THE BICYCLE

It hurtled from behind the sky,
it tore the sky in half—scraps—it roared,
I was with them—it came from nowhere—
two reeling petal-whorls of silver reeds strung to rip

the feathers from our throats, the wispy gasps,
the wind that pulled, there were flashes, gleams, smell of broken
earth, cold, the damp—no time—then gone, and the gash
sealed sudden as the hillside broke, sudden

the sky in shreds blurred its edges seamless—
and us left tucked together on the green, but frozen one and one and one
as if in winter swimming in formation on the pond
an instant ice no warning spread between us, held,

and all our bodies caught apart—no matter
for the moment—since then, apart.

I.

Forgot to say when. Forgot to stop
the clock. Forgot to draw straws.
Forgot to whisper words
that named. White ear. Woven

columbines in crowns around the horn.
Femur, fibula—Forgot the mirror.
Forgot the witness, tape recording
of the awe. Forgot to leave behind

the one who flicks the switch back on.
Forgot to analyze and notarize.
Forgot to hand the body
down. Forgot to count

the chores. Forgot the right hand
to cover the left heart. The sparkling
water. Forgot which eye, which ear, the starling's
call. Forgot to link the letters

of the chart to numbers. Forgot to knot
the rope. Forgot the code word
when the night hand reaches.
Forgot the entrance

to the tower. Forgot the compound
eye. Forgot biography. Forgot to count
the change. Forgot the faces
to remember. Forgot to answer

to my name. No division over zero.
Forgot to hold them responsible.
Forgot to hold them.

Here where the mark is having no mark.

Outside, the sun and the green hill shifting greens.
Outside, the sky. The green hills shifting.
The green hills rolling as the slow hand waves goodbye.

THE WINTER OF THE PRIMARY THINGS

Who could guess the ballerinas would be first to falter,
tutus drooping like plucked dandelions, the costumes

drained of color as if someone sipped pink
through a straw? The stage slumped from world
to planks and nails, the tidy thud of toe-shoes sputtering out
as if movement itself has been outstepped, and beyond, only

the paralysis of infinite finitude— In the air, the melody
dwindled, an open music box forgotten in the curtains,
the intervals stretching outward like the echo of last applause
before invisible hands folded back, before the sounds

could not sustain the space between the sounds
and the single tones, wholly themselves, drift out over the empty seats.

The thought: —it did not
know what the coil inside
that stretched it, all the sand grains
sorted through a sifter, the mesh
sky it fell through and landed:
thinking. The coiled thing rigged.

Just the grains nudged and no one
with the word for it. Some sprung on no
occasion and the still ones calling
"wind, wind" after the gone bodies,
"Hush, the outside made it
happen." And had they chosen

one to break. And had they lined
their clipboards, each one scribbling
the thought ahead, ahead, in time—
had the sun in shards within the monocle
converged to crisp the edges—and how
the splintered spill, and could it

speak the name had the bits of pattern
fumbled out? Had a flame sparked to
molecules of flame called "air" before
the forks converged again to smother?
And the sky, an accident of stems
split open, had the grass blades

breaking down the center spilt
each the wound blue molecule?
It was the first that did it: the breaking
grain, its fractured halves that broke
the ones around, who breaking broke—
The sun snapped from its elastic

cord and catapulting back, the shadow
cast itself on every side, the glass vial
tipped and from the center tendrils
lounging outward—   Noon again, and
creased like they'd remembered, the wires
tensed to hear the tuning fork.

We worshipped the animal by
cutting off his horns and grinding them

to bits of dust, which we contained
in small glass beakers. We worshipped

the animal when we unwrapped his inner
workings from his skin, peeled him

with special scissors, a sharp metal. Careful,
we kept his outline together that it might

still cast a shadow because what is volume
to a shadow?—We could have pegged

a half-skin to the light board—we could have
cut out ten animals from his own animal skin

and pegged them to the light board and
arranged them in a circle and said to him

and pointed with a pointer, Here,
here, here you are, all these animals you

never called by name. Do you
recognize? Do you hear me, dead ear?

THE ONLY YAK IN BATESVILLE, VIRGINIA

At first I spent hours gazing at the black and white horse
in the farthest pasture. He was so far away,
so tiny between the fence slats, and even then I knew
all he cared about was his mane and that his tail
was properly braided. He never so much as galloped
in my direction. Even the flies that edged
his beautiful eyes never flew into my wool
or landed on my nose. The love affair

was over before it began. I started to dream
of a dry cistern in the middle of the forest
and dry leaves where the other yaks could play
until leaves stuck out of their hair and they looked
like shrubs. In my dream they lived
in the cistern and each morning looked out
with periscopes before scrambling up the concrete walls
to search in the forest for sprouting trees.

In winter I realized that for the other yaks
it was fall all year round, and that it had to be fall,
because otherwise they couldn't roll in the leaves
to look like shrubs, and there had to be a cistern,
because otherwise they couldn't huddle in the pitch black,
and I knew then that I had forgotten
what a yak looks like, though I am a yak,
and I knew then that I had been away for a long time.

The Sheep Who Fastened the Sky to the Ground

After I found out that you were a sheep,
it was always afternoon, and I stood trembling
at the pasture fence, my hands full of dandelion
and the longer grasses. How could I call you

to come near? We had no names and only
this place, this sun, the hill and its limitless sky
held together by your gentle outline as you leaned
toward tufts of grass. How beautiful you were,

so still, so close to moving. I gathered
bouquets of clover, strung violets from the fence slats.
Sometimes I whispered, but the words disappeared
before I knew what they were or what they meant.

Once I saw darkness. I remember my eyes were open
and there was nothing, only black, and my heart aching
as I felt for my face and I was still human. While I cried,
stars came and traced sheep in the sky and the voice that knew

never spoke. I fell asleep mistaking the scent of hay
for your breath. To wake once from the sleep in which
you are held, in which your name emanates without utterance
from the being that cradles you—There is no other sleep.

Now it is always afternoon. How can I call you
when we have no names? I search
for the clover and violets. There are always enough.
My shadow is always the same length and shaped

with arms and legs. Between us, the distance of field is green
and exact; the sun gleams from its cloudless height—I know
that there is enough time, that there is always enough.
Please. Come to me, remember me: undo this world.

SWEETS TO THE SWEET

Farewell. The dead stand to applause, remember

each hour in analog, arc of an inch. The tableau

notched to scroll, thread the pupil, eye's hinge

nodding yes, yes, enough. The bluffed

eavesdropping on the day sky's aphasia—

Lest I'm left behind. Less than I

could count the bunched field flowers, crown or boughs

or stilled beneath the billowing, the hoary

lung's rusted inhalation. Riv-

ulet. Riven. The splintered sphere, anthelion where Gemini

mimes the doubled time, the un-sun's cameo

burned in profile on the blue. *Lest kneel,*

implore, mere coils the vulgar dust to rise—

No sigh—unstitch the willow leaves or covet

ease beneath the chordal surface: strings

slack. I guessed a table prepared. [Ex-

MID-AFTERNOON

The crane that measures the sky in triangles.
The lot that measures the earth in rectangles.
I would have killed her had the blood not rolled

over the property line, had the cough not called
me back, right fist and teeth and I thought it was the sun
glaring, had the whimper from the spilled body

not called me back. And the boy in green
running down the far hill and above him the diamond
on a string and the sky creased to be folded.

And in the field, the hay rolled in woven bales and spaced
like barrels pushed into the river and the river
tugging shapes on cords of current,

cords to hoist the curtains back. Like drifts of salt
left drying on the ocean flats, gulls chalk-scrawling the blue
sky and I in my sundress on the porch,

and in my beaded sundress. Needle that threads
the top of the head *up*. No—was not the *stop*
that caught me spotlight circle, posed body

a minute hand in the blank face. But the tangled head
a split end. But the un-knit chest a mess of fraying wires,
wicker hoop whipped with a stick down the dirt row.

SYNODIC MONTH

Moths rise from the pillow, dust-flutter
settling a shroud, powdered, and the wing hinge
shrieking, a pitch pulse that whispers—*Listen,*

the moths lay their eggs in our house—
We press to replay, we press again—the rock
thrown down the well, blank of the new moon,

black circle pasted on a black square.
Mandibles sharpened on rust.
We replay the voice that says:

(Rewind—splash of the thrown rock heard from
underneath—square of sound on the circle
of soundlessness.) Up. The new moon

scratches and black scabs scatter
from the black. We pull our blankets
to cover ourselves, but the moth-worms

are hatching, bodies empty as a windsock
on the moon. Give me your skin.
Rewind. *Give me your skin. Bodies*

empty as a windsock, a head's last imprint
on its pillow, white circle on a square of
white, blank tape running forward,

running backward. The mothers of the moth-worms,
here, fat from the attic. We dump the ashes
over the side of the boat, last words rising

to the surface. We screw the lid
back on. We unscrew the lid.
We dump the ashes over the side of the boat.

The rather mottled pig
who peeks between
the pen beams whispered,
"Count the pigs out
playing in the field
and come to tell me.
I will fashion a beret
of plantain that rims
the fence rows and crown
you piglet of the hardest
hooves." Easy, but

the pig who ran so fast
could have been himself
and the pig whose tail
he chased, could've been
the pig who hovered
with his hooflets outward,
a funny trick, or
maybe it was me?
I counted two, then
counted three. The vector
sum of pigs increased

as I approached, the blur
of legs and snouts, and
they themselves, however
many, chanted numbers
to each other, prime
numbers in four digits
was the pattern I perceived
before the wind shifted
and the pigs like tumbleweed
blew south toward
the equator.

II.

RELIQUARY

From the stone tower, the church bells quelled
their palindrome of hours,

but the black air fractured, the jagged masses nudging
and the jostled edge-dust

sifting to the manor gardens, down between the statues facing one another
gripping scrolls of stone,

lace cuffs in stone. Enough scuffing and a gap the width of the moon's
blade will splay,

hatchet straining on its shoelace. Square knot tied
through an eye. Enough

for the earth-dome to cave, cracked glass holding
the pressing system's well

of mercury in place, the lunar fingers loosening
the bind—

And behind the stride, a line of trampled
switchgrass, and ahead

the crickets spray to either side, a wake before the foot
stepped down, the stitch

of the earth clipped and the crickets' black bodies the thrown
threads sprung from the seam

—Here—space for the gash, drip, for the moon's black handkerchief
to drift initials downward

through the firs—the earth's unbreath, the still chest
unbuttoned on the ground.

The Bearing

The leak in sky smelled—vanilla-burn, the sickly sweet,
arrival of white procession for the bearing,
the rooster on the weather vane turning and turning his iron claw—

And the husks hull-split, the old kept air
dusting from within, each feather-seed
shuttled away

(and where it landed,
in the branchy shrub half-filled with fallen leaves, half
with birds of browns and reddish browns mixing)
(the push of bird-rustle from the hedge, the hum press, pulse)

(and where it landed, on the river currents braiding)

Before the petrified—the pore-pitted surging against.
And then the idea inside like a tugging. And then the tugging
away, the separate weights sorting each alone.

The wind chimes ring farther through the bronze tunnel of air,
and the gowns for the bearing shimmer, shuffling embedded sparkle.

Slowly the lungs fill,
a liquid nitrogen, so
the interstices of sky, shrieking, a plane of cold meets a plane of cold,
and at the pleat, cold—

the curled, crenulated feathers of the red leaf folding—

(And the leaves strung up like single letters inked and drying.)

And the color listening for call. The fallen
thing impaled on a jut of twiggy branches.
(Beneath the bark, the insects burrowing—)

(And more beneath, the earth organizing the arrangement of the
    blades, the soft
sorting, the placement here then here, here, the steady push—
The dirt beneath heaves the grass blades up in order toward the light,
or away

away, from underneath, up out of the ground's way.)

THE LAST CRWTH PLAYER

and if you remember, do you—and if

skin, lace ribbon, how slender the arm

between our bodies, do you remember

afternoon, that first, sun, field, dress, your

arm as I took your hand to my lips, how soft

the weight, the river's pizzicato, sound of a body

exchanged for another body, and if I held

a living, a new, and the ribbon

lace cuffs brushing your wrists, and if I longed

how you smoothed and folded, how your dress

swayed and your hands, and if

I wanted, the day, the sun over your shoulders

in the prairie of foxtail grasses and if and the prairie

of foxtail grasses, your shoulders, and the first

day, Dearest—may I call you—dearest—

Alabaster. Marble boy with the blood beneath—Years—
the layers and layers of stone. I lined
the shiny features on the tile for him. Bullnose chisel
struck with a lump hammer. Held him

while the shingles, while the ridges shivered open—I
wedged it in, deep so the fissures nerved. So to grind
the plates, the tangled channels yawning up. And have
the plaster fragments shatter. Free. And sweep

the fault dust out and excavate the residue with bristles.
Pores levered open with the fine-tooth marble claw.
I gave him water from the filter, scraps: the tinsel,
bunion bone, and the wads of foil—And underneath

the stone, the shivering. He coughed
ajar. He coughed and the nose drip and the eyes
from under wet lashes. Whisper, sweet boy,
lips a scarlet ribbon left on the hallway landing, ratchet

for the iron key. Wet-lashed. The jut filed smooth with the pumice.
And punctured holes, a 12-inch point, the tiny holes
struck along the hairline. Smooth with the riffler. When I
brush the temples—damp—and the filming eyes and the hands

unclasped. And underneath the shivering, the rasp—glass
boy, boy of cathedral bells, the silken filament leading
out— Sheath of rain from the gutter. And his shoulder
sockets, blades the armored plates, panels swung

on hinges—And the vertebrae curved, holes where the linings
shone, luminous. So clear the center, frozen gust. Trickle
of pump rust and the boat in ribbing from the keel, the ticking
vault—lissome, the lithe, weight of the frame, oh beautiful

body that lets my body sleep.

THE GUINEA PIG AND THE GREEN BALLOON

I approached the luminous stranger who came to me
from darkness in a gown of lettuce leaves, in a velvet

cloak of green that appeared at first another piece of dark,
but pulled apart into the glow-sphere that danced

in swaying steps, the lucent majesty that slipped toward me
from the reigning silence black above my cage.

Oh extravagant—and were my teeth too sharp to greet
or sharp enough? I do not understand now what was meant

to happen and what was a mistake—but know the bursting,
the sickening snap of ecstasy wrenched back to the body

and the green gown flung in crippled circles traced
like diagrams of wasting moons above my head—or portals

to another world, I thought, but as I thought, the shriek
dissolved, the body crumpled from the air and landed

on its side beneath the salt lick. All night I tended
the wasted skin and careful, brought it water,

alfalfa, made a bed of cedar chips and tried to gather
molecules of breath that floated from the plant shelf.

When I remembered morning, I began to cry, began to pray
for night to stay until the green took shape again

and if that shape were gone, I prayed for night
to stay, to be held in the same forever-dark

in which I first looked up and saw the gentle body,
and saw the graceful swaying of the stranger coming

as if for me—now I do not know—but then,
as if for me, and all my loneliness gone.

THE WALK

The woman came toward me through the woods with a hatchet.
She was coming through the woods with a shotgun.
The trees bent and swayed around the path,

a delicate canopy, the lake a dropped quarter behind
the brink. And the near-mute lap, tendril lick,

was it the lake—or lacy wings of butterflies leaping
from leaves? Oh, the least of these. She, brisk
with bullet holes, carrying a butcher knife.

"From those who have nothing, even what they have
will be taken away," I thought, as she walked tugging her examination
    gloves,

stainless steel stethoscope around her shot-through throat.
"For to all those who have, more will be given,"
I said aloud as she strode toward me in her leotard

and rapped thrice on my head with a cloth-covered brick.
I heard her count through the hole in her throat,

raspy as the crow-cackle grating from their roost
in the tall dead tree which moaned and creaked as it bent side-stitched,
its shriveled roots spread miles under the earth, miles to the water table

where the red and eyeless millipedes prune their poison sacs,
and outward wide as the woods where the mushroom hunters

hunt in the moist dew dawns. (She had me by a cord around my throat.
She had me in the net-and-pulley treetrap.) "Oh, to the least, to me,"
I wheezed, and pointed out the sun, still high in the sky, still spotted

with sun spots. I took her spotted hand in mine as we both looked up
    into the blue,
and the long honey locust pods rattled high in the honey locust tree.

The Large

And when and waiting for the body to emerge again from the bramble,
the others overgrown, [could smell the others], and the sawdust chips
sealed around the echo of the last horse-clatter, deserted bed picked
among the roots, the sharpened rocks that raged frozen from the dirt.
    Quiet
in the pebble traps—the others in the ivy, in the dense buzz along the
    lake-edge,
the vellum-skinned browning, egg-surfaced and puckered. Lake in the
    break
of mud. Where the earth caught on its breath. Where it caught pit-choked
    and gashed, down-
fissured and the sun wedged in. And the sky leaning on the penny groove.
And the stream leading from underbrush a trickle, whisper
of a name, disappear, the Long-Hair brushed (somebody brushed the
    Long-Hair)—

> *not always the smaller body that pours*
> > *into the larger—that empties—The large that longs*
> *to lay the body down—mouthed—*

The Long-Hair groomed—(could hear the grooming, scratch, muffle-tug,
root-torn and the rub, the surface shavings loosening to give)—groomed
till the glint, instants of it, sparked off. (Watched the others for the glint.)
No waving just the harness den-sewn while the cut tongues
grew their heads full for the weight. Top-heavy and leaning further
than the hold. Fall still. Lie still now. Pine needles. The soft full rot so the
    blooming
vessel retch the inside out, rainbow-laced in bursts on the green (could
    hear,
could hear—) The sheerness drifts from the body then, (the others
unclasp the clasp, the softest pressure, bare hiss), single dull
click the slow billow, the followdown, the fold begins from the shoulders

III.

THE GIRLS

As our reward, she cut for the girls the nervous ribbon.
The figurines nearby filled with food the girls didn't want.
And the tire in the stream and the shoe hidden
inside the tire and the sludge hidden inside the shoe.
To make a home for the girls in the fern-forest where the brambles arched.
And stickers of the animals.

She read to the girls and the girls behind the outhouse
burying our talents. Slits
in the ground, the vent
closing up Venetian. Valved.
The crayoned Valentines filed in the slot machine.
Behind the warping
and the poison red berries from the hedge.
And the girl-song written by the girls.

She was handing out the flashlights and the batteries, then the stranger
loves the girls more.
The air so stiff, stream-clogged.
He gives the girls the guns to choose, which girl of
which of you, the girls with the guns against each the other's girl-heart.
I was standing by her first, then the stranger
loves my sister more. My sister with the gun against my heart.
Only the birds eat these berries, not the girls.
Only the birds with their mouths smeared red, with their bird-mouths
    puckered.
The birds fill their mouths.

Quota

I keep my dirty fingers in my mouth.
My tooth and my jaw and my neck. And my fever.
I have already taken the pain relievers.
Enough to fuel his exhibition, to stopper his syringe,
the neck with fluid pouches so the breath like a purr pushed through.
So the hum like a kitty-knocker.

We prod behind her Cartesian coordinates
as indicated. Adapted from his demonstration, the grid
over her face strapped with leather belts and silver buckles.
Polished silver dipped in vinegar.
And poke holes B and H through with a penknife.
M and U with a corkscrew.
I undid her garters and poked

at the holes it made there.
Handwoven by organic farmers.
Her swollen throat bulging at the razor.
If we all drank a good beer and had a good laugh.
If we all hugged 'round like a bear
and fed the lost pup vittles. I called, called, chisel

with a cloth-dulled hammer.
Sweat from her hour in the fester-hive.
I dipped my fever in the river
and it returned with my father before me, and before him, his.
The gimlet-head and mandibles bored deeper in
behind the ear. Pouch of air in the tendrils. I talked.
I talked like a dirty dirty fox.

And sometimes the strap-holes
like a perforated tin piece for the candle light,
like I could see the stars he punched
for me in the sky with his straight pins,
and sometimes the toothache. And the girl-whine.

And how the soup they'd pour
down my throat with a funnel
and how they'd slap me and shout how
I couldn't ruin this for them,
I couldn't ruin it. At the beading exposition

I watched him bead and heard his explanation.
And envied for his cookie.
And envied for his sick-claw every time,
the orange burlap throw-toy, collar of bells,
and for his hardbacked grammar
and for his mule that pulls and pulls
until the land dries up again. Doll rattle.
Chord bellows with a poker strapped to it.

Blood Weight

Collecting the torn paper collecting the rocks the glued-on fur

I send him a sticker and want him to take me

I weave the nesting flax the hair the dampened leaves I dipped them

(Musk oil, spermaceti) subterranean convolutions, the writhing begets

Next dosage delivered by parcel—passed through the needle eye—stop

With the crying / slap—in the gap that's where my crying is and he

Already on the other side not hearing pole vaulting away

Glitter necklaces / kazoos / the fun sack race with the friends

And me before, scrambling with my hands trying

To keep the separate tears corralled not the bride not

The handmaiden of the bride I

Saw him on the trampoline shrieking with the mail-ordered pouches

I saw him through the log in my eye my brain with a log

Me dragging and the speck in my brother's brain removing (me)

My tin can full of nails plaster-flaked my blight grater

Lamp rusted out with the drizzle (bulk) the dark left

Arrives in my sleep when the caked palm when the flattening comes

Still it (dull this dull it now) the flesh gut the tangle

How to stand w/ the lop and how to stand enough (to gather)

They told me said they promised the crying will stop when I'm better no

Broken-jawed mule broken crown no ladybug with only three dots

The rot abscess, rancid pocket with the fish bones wish

CINCH SONG

To the forest where he lay　himself among the leaves
and would not call　my name. The rusted door
in the cistern shaft　wailed on its hinges. My head
in the dark chimney　opened itself and the song
came out. Buried in　the leaves. I looked for minutes,
each leaf on the ground,　each spotted beetle sauntering
up tree trunks. Oh brittle　branches, he could be so still,
white sky empty of birds,　the sun and moon white

circles beneath all that white.　I tried to remember. Day
a rewound clock with golden　gears. Day the china doll
propped on the hall's glass table,　cracked ear the draft,
niche where the bees slipped　past to dance the ice hymn
in that head-hollow, wax-nest.　The gust a signal for the terrapin
to begin its plodding cross,　for the willful lost: be found.
I whistled and no one　whistled back, echo a whittled
hole in the air, leaf-sheaves　creaking, chink where the dirge

slipped past to stomp the dirge-　dance in curled moustache and bright
black boots. Come, wive me　to the fern-drag, the swollen
stump in lichen, moss rocks　plush to hem the bleat
in, muzzle of dirt, muzzle　of trees. The trap breeze-tripped
and the leaf pit—He fit　perfect. Stagnant as the brackish
last water that hummed stench　from the cistern hole. Gloss
of a sheen of a glaze of a　blank. To bide the time. Ocean
bride that waves charades to play　the unbreathed words cleaved

from sound. Oh body, cleave　to the ground's verge, the surge
of honeysuckle—veil of moor-　grass, veil of stone and ivy.
It's the buzzing head that threads　the box seams, the black hawk-spots
sky-caught to knot the long　spill of days still—Dazzled.
I looked for minutes, each linnet　song-spaced behind leaves, thief
of a vision, the gaunt siren　shrouded on its branch. Quenched
when the nail drove home, quill-　pierced shriek the shrill aria
to the sick-ear. Feather blight.　Scratched groove tied to replay.

THE TERM

My clock is fast. I don't know how fast. I wanted
to be with him on the glacier, just the two of us
freezing and turning away from each other in our ice bed
while the floe droned south, inexorable. My swelling cycle

with the moon, my gibbous. It's not
a flattering light. Somebody would have been
better off without, and I'm certain it's me, but we've
already pushed off with a paddle toward the main-ice, all the colors

kept under. Six feet deep. I stepped over it
the first time, sheer luck—make room for me. A door
to the rubble. So as not to interrupt the dark pulse, *no
difference, no difference.* So as not to disrupt the blossoming

litter, their tiny digits. Sometimes the rootless chasm-bridges—
top-shards snatched by the antarctic winds, gambled, cast
like pick-up sticks—can't be distinguished
from the surface, cannot hold the weight.

Even the delicate-pawed cadaver dogs . . . they
have learned from someone other than me
not to flinch. Not to drop the mementos down the ice-maw.
A trail in the ice scrub leading. His scribble:

Momentous: the bulbous hatched today, a halo of babies.
I saw a map of me, the ground not to scale. Light strapped on the head
where the third eye would open. Just that they be
synchronized, his breath recorded in ice, his voice a pigment

in the tendrils of ice algae. I didn't write the obituary
and by then I'd forgotten. Blown-glass birds on the windowsill
sending rainbows in scattered patterns around the makeshift
kitchen, our hut for observation. Other women

grown for concubines. He could freeze it off,
or freeze it off. No magnifying glass to see the babies closer.
The babies spilling from the tapered end of the tear, I'd thought
a rupture from the swell, I'd thought it would

burst me please. If only the old others were here, if
the others. The dogsleds padlocked to the chain
nailed with a stake into the ice. For shame, he would say.
And I *am*. On all fours, I'm all for it.

When it's time to move, he takes me for a walk.

Sometimes we go into the other room and sometimes into the kitchen.

When we pass by the mirror, he points in at the collar—polished, so the
    metal sparkles.
She's always there, very quiet.

Sometimes I look at her but only when he points. I must,

except when the eyes weigh down so the lashes touch and the body
folds itself fan-wise

    creased out of napkins like in the red booth when my father took us
    and taught us the words in French, when it was the tree with the
    blossoms like pink-fringed feathers and the paintbrush

He jerks on the chain as a reminder. He used to make up stories for her.

Before the fits. Before the sobbing that took up the space

so he couldn't breathe in his favorite chair, the green one. Cried her

swollen body still. And the trembling still.

    My beautiful quiet girl.

Once I said his name like a question, and he walked away
into the other room and shut the door.

There are two
rooms. The room where I'm kept in the evening, to be quiet

while he works, tapping and tapping on the keys and laughing
out loud and telling stories when the phone rings and he answers it

because it's someone from the outside. The outside, always
swelling and fumbling and searching, when we are so safe here, warm,
    and the window blinds down.

Then, the room where I'm kept
in the morning. Where the pillows are and the heater billowing and
    fogging.

And the desk I looked in once, an accident, and the pictures
of strangers like me there, forty or fifty, cut out of magazines
and pictures of strangers like him, cut out of magazines.

At first, he played
the songs for me and I would sing and wear the outfits.

And spin to his knees from the far corner, and how I would hold him
    then, how I would hold him—

Some days he takes me in the elevator

        and the 3 in a circle with the light behind it

To the room with machines to build the strength back up. The doorman

keeps the big room empty for us. He bows to me in his uniform.
He sees her. She has a wide satin ribbon tied around her throat.

My beautiful girl, your throat

like a Parmigianino

    (like in the afternoon when he came to me, when with his cuffs
    unbuttoned I kneeled to his wrists and the cathedral bells through
    the window a scarf that wrapped us together and the day a blue
    square that led to the piers splintered with boats, light-strung and
    wreaths on the masts

Home
is the button with the number 7. My favorite number is 73,

and my favorite animal is the dolphin. And the green planets
I cut out of paper and lined with wires in orbit. He does not

hear me when I speak. I said to him, Green is my favorite color too.

THE DUSK HARUSPICY

Organic matter burning in the swamp, the great wasp

snarling at the shreds of paper hive— The glow-ring rising

from the vast decomposition, will-

o'-the-wisp,

the live thighs slit and filled with scalding oil. The beatings

overseen—(Silent the new moon, dampers on the sky-strings

down.) Oh my

phosphorescent—

And recruits distributing the pamphlets. What is it

wants attention from the gnats? Wanting

for the breath, the grass a list of evidences?

(The ear bones accounted for,

two by iron instruments of shaping, and last where the spur

suspended for the flank-jab hangs—) This, this deed

built into the posture, and the posture spent. Snapped

and the hacking

begins, beetles glistening in the hot centers of the flowers,

a crown of wishbones to be fitted. White bones,

white— Inchworms crushed by the medicine ball. Somebody

call "time."

That he may bed them under there in the lost river.

Understitch, ear-licked, and the gnomon casting its angled

omen over the Roman nine. The next an X.

The burials proceeded.

IV.

Night Shift

I'm putting the fuel cylinders in the broken rocket.
I keep putting the new ones in, taking the old ones out,
grime on my sleeve, my
sleeve, I
haven't slept for seven days, regalia stained
with gasoline, the wings
askew and the cockpit empty. Seven days and
seven— Nights spent
chronicling the shades
of dark—(the dark
that fills my brain, my mouth, my
heart, the second chamber of my heart, marble
tile where the shift did fall— And the geese
rising from the long grasses at the edge—
and the star pulse—)

And in mine heart the rope-chafe and the burn, sternum
a pulled badge, clasp-mangled.
And when I was done.
And when I woke—asked me, pressed the yes
button: hinge-jaw
glutted with the macadamia. Dropped me off at the rocket station
with his face peeling off and the other face
underneath, I saw it in the peel-waves, when the shuttles
flashed by, star-streaked, and breezed the peel aside. My

mouth parched here with the oiling can and the gas can. I
thought the crowd closed in, the breathing
tight, the hole sewed up to a tiny, filled with ash.
Ash egg for the smoke screen.
Ash on the head of a pin. He hid

his hands where were they.
He held up numbers behind his back and wouldn't
answer when I guessed. The ropes
embedded in. My hands so cold
I couldn't thread it, couldn't, fell open, gash in the
side and a slice to attract
the insects, maw
with its list, the paddle blades balanced
on the webbing.

What do I deserve.
The takeoff lineup counting down in integers.
His hands under a rock pulling more rock down. The silver
bullet in the gullet.
The miniature ponies outside, so small,

with high whinnies and kneecaps ready to splinter.
I begged them on my tiny knees.
I begged them with my jewel case open, the velvet pouches, drawers of
    mirrors
and the hooks where the filigree necklaces, diaphanous—

Then, invisible tape to fix the face back on,
pockmarked in the scrub garden harvesting the nightshade.
Beyond the wall
a hand tossed me
bread soaked in bouillon, spittle
laced for a doily— My head
aches, in my heart with the hornets
coming down. Sear upon my thigh.
The second eyelid—transparent—

(But the lightning bugs that rose from the field,
light buoys stung in the black, pin-fastened to make the volume *there*,
the air over the field—and the space
real, a place to pass through, to
strap the sandals on   silently for it is night and the mother
        asleep in her silks
                and the rabbits quiet in the felled stalks.)

CRYPTOGRAPHY

When the people talk
I hear them all the same.

The fridge door
open and water pouring

down the tile. Where the piece
fits, where the lisp,

where they laid the body down,
shovel, the stone—I'd

chew through my own
phone cord to get to the

Blank. Filament that carries
like a body the voice of the body—

A bolt of skin for the men
of the Black Chamber—quill it in

demure with fur
in the jeweled miniature. I'd

dig a hole the size of my brain.
I'd dig a hole to cover up

my coughing. Water
under the rug, breath

in the acorn caps. A zero
with one hundred zeros after.

The quarter's nailed down
to the porch. Behind the hedge,

the hedge pig whimpers, stick
leaned up against the shed.

THE FOIST GRID

Beneath the hour, the door on sprung
hinges. The pendulum a fanning of cards behind which

the blank is switched and what inhabits it
switched. What, to appear in the space of its

expelling. A crow on the highest roof's highest jutting pipe.

Someone had to go into the earth for this to happen and that
behind it, someone was under the earth and the dirt

was in someone and the hole where the dirt was.

And the blood of the land soaked up. The bad cocoons drowned in
    alcohol.
The wormhole and the catacombs scanned
for someone surfacing. The sun

has been busy in its burning. A shadow to its wall
like a film.

The square days exchange the blank between them
and pass beyond then. A matrix. An inheritance

of blank, the others looking
at their watches and the hours with their doors to enter.
The others breathing it in clear

and exhaling it fogged.
Oh how the blood peeled away and behind it what, a space
in which to shift something

new? The groaners press the panel in the tree trunk then
and disappear. The others approached removing their helmets.

And beneath their helmets, a wide flat rock
and beyond the rock, the sea.

QUEEN REGENT QUEEN REGNANT

Lack of gum to fill the machine,
fly wings for the papier-mâché
head, mural of pompoms stuck with spit—

I took the escalator up, the escalator down.
I picked up buttons from the ground
and placed them in a jar without

a label. I swept the onion skins
from her table and put them in a sack
I tied with strands of leather

braided to a string. (She deserves it
for her fling with the boy who played
third trombone in Oklahoma City—)

I looked left, then I looked right.
I swabbed the pods of blight
from the leaves of the broad-leafed fig.

I swabbed the dust that gathered
on the paint-by-number. The specimens
in the chamber were withdrawn discreetly

using forceps, borscht steeping on the Russian
stovetop. I intercepted precepts
on my radio decoder and placed the telescopic data

in a sprung manila folder. She
called out from the kitchen, "Oh, the soup
is growing colder. Won't you come

re-light the pilot light you doused
with rubbing alcohol?" Witch hazel,
I snarled, and No. (She deserves it

for the row of beetle husks I lined
upon the sill which she disturbed,
and for the pills she tries to slip

into my coffee.) I used the calipers,
cosecant, and the friction index
to determine the equation. The viscous

combination bubbled in the calibrated
cylinder. By law of laboratory
etiquette, I wafted with my hand

then retrieved the envelope
dated 1986. Time to mix— Time
to fix the stitches of that balsa

finch, intervals of wind chimes
aligned by the golden triangle.
Love, your maniacal—but first

to wash my hands—my hand, my
other hand—And the landscape:
termite dunes, the carving ants

that carry leaf shards down the trunk;
the schoolboys run in kneesocks
through the field, each his kite

unwinding from the handled
spool, the sky in parallelograms, the line
of boys, the javelin.

HOURGLASS

The body watermarked and held
to light—metal grain of rice

embedded fast behind the ear. For should
it wander. For should it net

its shadow on the water,
a doorway etched by light the body blocked—

Frames the space the body fits. Perfect. Yes
and the ink stamp

and the char test and the dipped
in ammonia, gear teeth ticking.

Treadmill where the tethered
in a running wheel, where the tethered

in a crevice, egg timer soft
to sift. The motor shifts

the current underwater. The motor
by the cumulus the nimbus and the cirrus,

fan blades and the spaces separating
starlings on the wire— And the leak

swirled up from smokestacks underneath, green rings
shimmering around the throats. It's the ghost

of myself begs. The clover plowed under. Let it
with the floating pier away. And with the running river

miles into the flattest horizontal, the barley fields
and mules that mouth their timothy bales, the grain-shift

quiet in the silo-shaft. Rat
nudging at the night. The no-light pressing soft

the body loam into the ground. An orphan in the rafters.
An orphan folded like a fruit bat in the attic window.

Transporter

Oh raw, raw—
They send me out on an errand for the words.
They send me out to switch the samples and the charts.
You, who are marked for this coincidence.

And if I stopped moving like sometimes the sky tells me.
And if I stopped moving like sometimes the weight of the walk, like all
    the separate materials
in their separate jars, primary and ignorant.

The winged girls appeared then by the Susquehanna selling electronic
    wares and digital wares.
In their silver head wraps, and with wrists braceleted with thin silver
    hoops, they lined
the black plastic pieces on an observation podium for the onlooker to
    consider.

And will we go swimming then when the waters are warm. And will we
    swim
before they detonate the three-mile island. The glow-ring with its
circumference expanding in shock concentrics

and the populace running, clogged
against the bodies of the populace running.

The carillonneur tugs the ropes for the separate bells in order.
Somewhere the sandwiches are wrapped in plastic and tucked neatly
    under the boat seat.
Somewhere the canned pear-halves, the smog-sided buildings
hunched in the urine and the vomit.

And in the warm waters, and will
the waters be warm?
Water, i.e., a metal spigot sticking from the earth like a lance reamed
    through.

The money was to see the angel joints move on their own silvery hinges.
The exchange of tiny discs of ice.

It's not natural but it's natural for long enough. I trust that you will wake
    me in time.
I have to get home, you see. I have to fix the engine.
The light is glowing at least I can say the light is glowing.
Thin as a wire, then who comes dancing with the shears—the reeds

grown out of the whisper to whisper it again in the wind.
The basilica filled with light, light pouring through the stained glass station
    windows.
One of us will open up the earth for the other of us
and then seal it behind.

The Secret Arsonist

Even the birds clustered in the red
maple, dragonflies
fingers that file the blame-
less from
the blamed, coin slots
for eyes—
what if the cardinals, what
if the cut
tongue of Saint John Nepomuk
thrown
from the bridge, red garter
of the Queen?
Almost the enchanted come to make
good—ace
of diamonds the heart turned
inside-
out, heart turned its back on the ax-
is—only
the abacus, wooden beads chiding
the divisor.
Wind chimes tally from the scaffolding
—Seamless
the kiosk, keys, the tossed coin still
exchanging
face for carving underneath a face,
scarves
waving from the tower, coat
of arms
the unanimous vote cast, the stacked
masks
shaping the word—faster—fast till
only the mouth
only the word of the mouth—

At the train station, two men
stand in
the granite, glint where the five
clocks cross
faces—hat on the head,
hat
in the hand. The man unfolds
a penknife
from the paper towel. The man
in the orange
suit brushes with turpentine—
Line
of passengers—pass to the
left, face
to the left. The man with the hole-
punch in
his pocket, pin through the hip, man
who staples
behind glass, duct tape on the cuff
of his sleeve.
A finger presses the button,
the quotient
is zero, sleep is the sound
left over,
another train vanishing into
a rhyme
of itself. The letters flutter in their
slots. Destinations
changing. The indexed names
are falling
off the tickets. The time is one minute
behind. Blank 1:
I choose. Blank 2: I choose I.

First the tousled reeds soak
themselves
in kerosene. First the piccolos
whet
their tongues against the metal.
The breaths
are counted in their canisters. Someone
will allot
the number. Someone will align
the tassels,
the man with gloves for hands, pins
pursed
in his mouth. Rubber shoes coax
the rewound
measures from macadam, sound
enters
at the ankle, whir of the scolex,
embroidered
vest—Underneath, the teeth keep
time, new
seconds under the snapped
polyester,
each woodwind line a measure
behind—Run
until the lag, into, features flagging from
the faces, always
the initial breath, melody about to hit
the high
note, throat, the thrown baton hovering
in air—Down-
beat, Up. The needle is stuck.

At the end of a glass eye—Omens—
Only the cold
echoes: the bride streaks down
a castle
corridor, her trailing veil
the ice-tail
of a comet etched in black
linoleum.
Perfume rises from the portrait
necks, glow
from the polished oak a slow
bleeding
from beneath the fingernail—
The sheets
have waited. When will the hornets,
when from
the tangled orchard arms like a dark
tiara? Girls
lead by a ribbon in the frozen
rows. One,
a kaleidoscope in her pocket; one,
glass beads on a string. Posed, the earth holds
the moon
from its face—eye looking back
on the black
socket. How can you say—mine?

SECRET ARSONIST

The cradle sings a lullaby with
five teeth
missing. Trial one: phone
dialed
by the wrong hand, the sleeping
man his own
forged signature. The mark
surfaces,
names scrawled in iodine
on the backs
of corn husks— Two: the contour
map, graph
of how the tariff rose for sleep-
lessness,
ears to hear the wire fraying—
I'm awake,
traffic guided by the handbell
choir, the crucial
dropper designating virus to a vial:
corked—
Quintuplets switch their rattles
on the latchhook,
sleeves flay the collar on the clothesline—
Time—Look
under your canopy bed. Look again.

V.

empties again, and again the scratching at the onset
the squirrel claws scrambling across the brick across the shagbark
the moths indoors still clutching to the flowered print
their brown stiff bodies clutching, the tiny moth feet into the panel dug
we are lost we dare not move
like tiny shingles papering, the mica laminae disjointed
scabbed and the pixelled static bestrewn breath-bound elsewhere—
sketched isosceles and at the vertices the wingtips dusting
and at the vertex-odd the mandibles shivering while in the sky the colored
    gliders swallow-dōve
we know not the how to keep us how to stay the wait, we stay
for home made by the coat being hung
for there were times, in the thicket, with the child asking for her pail back,
before we were flushed within, the gone away gone without hitting any
    surface
the moon a wax seal melted over the lip where the sky would say—
we hear not the call to the eye the water hole to stow away we are lost
the shavings of my heart and the synth skin-
tone to match, gray triangles ragged on the edge, sketch
for the centerpiece, and the starfish sludge-gasped and the whorl, the
    message,
gnawed into the attic and rattling there, cheeks full of leaves
we dare not move we smell not the burning of our god we know not
and how to bury one without the other falling, sleeping
hook for the weight, and in the lavender room, and where the line is, and
    where
the break in the flesh, where the other lingers
time-screen torn, and the will intoxicated on the thirst, and the thirst—

RENT

But from the outside it seemed
an acquisition, the populace confused by a hanging garden.
—The bucket full

then too full. Then overflowing completely
into nothing, call it
a new hour, the bells starting over. Each injured animal

accessible in the petting zoo; one limping.
One with mange. Others you could not tell
what was wrong exactly, but then,

there they were. Crenels and merlons like a queen's crown.
Except dulled flat, like a queen.
There were no such invitations to the surf nor also to the picnic,

the month coming to an end, and the cash cow dry in the udder.
It's been difficult to navigate my country
not speaking the language of my country.

Only a few more washes of the silverware.
Only a few more chargings of the nighttime dogs.
It will be a long life, I sometimes think, over my rind of melon.

I look then in my guide for the correct name to call it.
Some sentinels converge and diverge in varying formations.
A grocery bag blows by.

I want to present them with my shovel, but at last
know better, having learned something
from the pamphlets for God's sake; the pamphlets.

The prettiest balloons light purple and dark purple,
and the eulogist in passing
having tied one to my wrist—There was proof of him

having been in the sea, I could taste
the sea salt in his salty hair. It was time not
to alphabetize the shelves again. The shelves of everything shelved.

In the Third Hand

In the third hand, I placed the tame bird that comes from the gondola, he
that receiveth that he may be still always. The bird

who with the marbles rolling past.

The bird who, perched on slanted channels
where the sunbeams cast away backwards to the source, or,

random out in rays, and the dusky—(fog, smoke from the burning)—
    slithers in

coiled, the huddled maelstroms ready to constrict around a fallen thing.
An accidental loosening. Shipyard echoes. And the marbles

tumbled beneath the heavy lips of bells to tip them into
voice, the side-spill, and collision the sound. And abrasion

the echo left of the sound fallen

away from the hollow, away toward he that receiveth, he

my brother, the bird strung with ribbons.
To the tree, he circles back with the black box flashing, the rectangle of
    light
shifting in blue. And beneath, the mangled scrub roots arched.

East bath filled with mud. This is his brother, I, do you know

where he is. I and my friend my brother who perform the show
of silhouettes, his shadow

measured, pooled in disc against the grass?
Musty saucer for the cup of sky, prepared. A pattern pinned
aloft on the green blades, still

for the cut. Exact. The tender grass-shafts the table

for the timepiece, he whose wings
sewn on a pinwheel. This day, do, before the sun

measures the sundial black. Something to hold

the water for his bath. To stir the wind to spin. And then

into the after-hours, a pooling to lap the dark equilibrium, the shape
and rise, and then ahead the spill into the ditch.

WHAT ANIMAL

Even in the daytime
the swabs of cloud
approach lower, lower,

the sky mixing in more grey, more grey
it is never the right color, the desired

what animal has a coat of the desired color.

The bridge strung up, suspended by its arms and arms and legs and legs,
its body the weight dragging,
foghorn blaring from the port, across, on the edge of the land,
blackbirds that cross the rooftop signal,
blackbirds rising at once
and their rising the signal to rise,
over the rooftops in a chain-link mesh,
mercury beads on the streaks the purple air weaves in,
mercury beads squeaking on the glass of grey air—

what glass animal smolders
what animal smokes from beneath his coat of embers—

—unable to rise but able to count the numbers and the weight that piles
and the hours become the pillows underneath whispering sleep here,
    sleep it away

what red animal in the sleeper car
what volcanic ash

The color of the forest dampens.
At the center, the stone,
and at the center of the stone—

Listen to me, I said.
(Wishing well with the ivy from the mouth growing.)

(Does the mind lie among the leaves here waiting, is it
still, is it still enough, the body
of the hollow bell,
does the mind swirl among the no-sound and the no-sound swirling?
The none and none a double helix runged by light seeping into the tower
through the arched windows, the vent above, through the pores of the
    brick mortar.
The pestle-grind of the molecules of sky seeping and the blue dust,
the air scaling down the air, into air.)

the paring of the needs down to one, and what

ice animal
the center a puncture that spilled
the center a star explosion, frozen
flash of light, a burst

First the nerves, (the layered transparencies,
one on top of the other), then the organs, skeleton, then
the muscles, the skin, first
the dirt, then the dirt, then the dirt, the dirt,
then the dirt spilling from the inside.
Breathe into my mouth.
Let the dirt fall into my mouth from your mouth

What animal can be built from the dirt.

PASTORAL

The dark lambs trampled over the quilt of paisleys and flounces,

the quilt over the body where it lay.

The dark lambs trampled, their clover pastures nipped to the quick,
dirt in their muzzles as they nudged there, wondering.

Behind the lambs the castle burned and the moat glistened slick with
    gasoline.

Behind the lambs the paper cranes folded themselves a parachute to
    catch the wind.

There is only room enough for one still body in the bed.

When the body is carried away the bed becomes lighter.

When the rings and golden teeth, when the gold pin through the hip,
when the gold stone in the pit of the blood sack is taken away, the body
becomes lighter, the body can rise from its trappings, spread

like a mist over the fields like a hot air balloon rising
with its flame jetting and its sand bags tossed, and the grains like a mist

drifting from the bags as the bags drift, up over the fields
where the dark lambs trample in their fury for the flowers.

Up where the silver mobile rotates in the clouds
with its trinkets of tears, the dark tears tarnished on the dark wool.

The woman who cards the wool—
the dark lambs lick the salt from her

softly underneath the web of night, softly as the sand sifting down.

The dark lambs nuzzle from her palm.

You here, underneath the golden dome, the cinquefoils, and the fluted
pilasters,

underneath the windows fanning like a peacock's tail and the windows
arching like a peacock's plume,

is it you that's waiting for your bride?

Land Transaction on the Grass Swathe

And the documents burning with my old name burning.
A crude beveling with a hatchet and a swatch of bark to smooth the planks.
Rope and pulley, the mechanism set—
Exercised relentlessly until the dawn

and you upon the ground, you upon the ground.

And kneel beside the fallen overcoat and knot its empty sleeves

and wring its empty sleeves till the teeth fall out.

The hide scraped clean with a sharp rock. You'll reveal
for a small fee, as you put it, some recompense as you put it.
I used the safety matches first, and now have only
unsafe matches left. The cattle unnatural

with their front legs sewn together and their back legs sewn together.

Sometimes, lowing, they toppled over slowly like sheets

of plexiglass the better to lie on their sides.

Singing to one another between the hollow grass blades.
Sometimes someone catches an eye. My occupation to extract
the lucent honeysuckle nectar, the flower pinched

from the bottom and the drip swelling out.

The heavy bead bearing from the delicate funnel
downward. How pleasant to see the land from this angle,

underneath it. I thought perhaps if I gathered

the sugar drops if I let the sphere swell on its acanthine follicle its
transparency of plastic lanyard spun out like a
glass-thread pulled— I thought perhaps I could
light for you your cigarette.

If I shadowed your eyes with my eyes.

I thought perhaps you cried yellow tears and we agreed I would not

go home, no, neither of us want me to go home.

And now in the blue its tail-diamonds shimmering its body holding the air
to shape, specific volume, and the air with its brooch, hoisting it up
for the sun's engraving.

So, thinner and thinner—

And the western snowy plovers at the brink of wet sand, and where the
   coiled wave unrolls
the western snowy plovers singly wading, hesitant forward, the wave
   having thinned to its white
lining and folded under, the hem on its elastic current, back

withdrawn, and the snowy plovers, and the high grasses
in the dunes beyond, behind, their nests in the grasses.

And the sun with its cut, the long kite let out, string

engulfed by the blue, invisible, the line from the earth unraveling, and the
   spool
from where the line revolves away, the axis rotating,

the spool giving its weight and the body, so, thinner
against the blue. Here. Suspended.

And the body from which the kite
emerged, a flapping from the broken chest and away with a string
to tie the coil back

and the lines around the eyes, the lines beneath the eyes
and the grass in the far dunes swaying.

The body upright from the sand like a shard wedged in

and the wave licking the edge of the land
clean, the dirt into the ocean, the body of the land

pulled, and underneath the dunes, from where the long grass grew,
and among the slender roots, what made the land bulge,
what broke the chest to bulge—

or from above, around, what
moved the surfaces to hold, what filled, I

waited beyond the dunes, over, still and the kite motionless.

And the plovers.

TERCETS FOR THE END OF TIME

When it was the end of time, everything was beautiful
and big. Big obvious beauty like a honk. The huge glass pieces of sky
shaped like stalactites dripping liquid in an act of freeze.

Inside the operative wound, beneath the stitching
the music box had been sewn, and within that
the pocket watch on its tarnished chain. And inside that,

the great fire. The dragonflies failed
to agree upon their iridescence. And the birds called
again from the tower. The building of ribs where

the procession languished, and the soot on the ribs.
They hang the lanterns on a tree and strike them.
And smote the smoky glass. The asp within its asp-hole

waited. The vial it coveted filled— An extract
from a flower center, from the paws of bees? From the humming
throat of the kingfisher? From the glass-blown birds swirled

with colored glass inside the clear, and the glass fishes mounted
on pinnacles of glass? The sea glass in from the frustrated ships
in shades of brown and green and blue and clear . . .

The birds flew up out of the tree leaves like the shape of the tree
rising from itself, two panes of glass sliding over one another,
and from within, the skeleton of black dots rising,

rubbing over in an inky swoon.
A beautiful thing emerged from the beauty
of the earth, and of the air, and of the sea, and everywhere beheld.

I asked it, what is the name for the purple-flowered bush
where all the butterflies go to fan their yellow wings on the exhale?
It grew late then; the sky turned more and more blue

and the blue darkening. The blue a pressed bleeding between.
I could smell its lilac wispiness and the lilac of its whisper.
The bush is called "the butterfly bush," it said. It began to sing.

THE CONTEMPORARY POETRY SERIES
Edited by Paul Zimmer

Dannie Abse, *One-Legged on Ice*

Susan Astor, *Dame*

Gerald Barrax, *An Audience of One*

Tony Connor, *New and Selected Poems*

Franz Douskey, *Rowing Across the Dark*

Lynn Emanuel, *Hotel Fiesta*

John Engels, *Vivaldi in Early Fall*

John Engels, *Weather-Fear: New and Selected Poems, 1958-1982*

Brendan Galvin, *Atlantic Flyway*

Brendan Galvin, *Winter Oysters*

Michael Heffernan, *The Cry of Oliver Hardy*

Michael Heffernan, *To the Wreakers of Havoc*

Conrad Hilberry, *The Moon Seen as a Slice of Pineapple*

X. J. Kennedy, *Cross Ties*

Caroline Knox, *The House Party*

Gary Margolis, *The Day We Still Stand Here*

Michael Pettit, *American Light*

Bin Ramke, *White Monkeys*

J. W. Rivers, *Proud and on My Feet*

Laurie Sheck, *Amaranth*

Myra Sklarew, *The Science of Goodbyes*

Marcia Southwick, *The Night Won't Save Anyone*

Mary Swander, *Succession*

Bruce Weigl, *The Monkey Wars*

Paul Zarzyski, *The Make-Up of Ice*

THE CONTEMPORARY POETRY SERIES
Edited by Bin Ramke

Mary Jo Bang, *The Downstream Extremity of the Isle of Swans*
J. T. Barbarese, *New Science*
J. T. Barbarese, *Under the Blue Moon*
Cal Bedient, *The Violence of the Morning*
Stephanie Brown, *Allegory of the Supermarket*
Oni Buchanan, *What Animal*
Scott Cairns, *Figures for the Ghost*
Scott Cairns, *The Translation of Babel*
Richard Chess, *Tekiah*
Richard Cole, *The Glass Children*
Martha Collins, *A History of a Small Life on a Windy Planet*
Martin Corless-Smith, *Of Piscator*
Christopher Davis, *The Patriot*
Juan Delgado, *Green Web*
Wayne Dodd, *Echoes of the Unspoken*
Wayne Dodd, *Sometimes Music Rises*
Joseph Duemer, *Customs*
Candice Favilla, *Cups*
Casey Finch, *Harming Others*
Norman Finkelstein, *Restless Messengers*
Dennis Finnell, *Belovèd Beast*
Dennis Finnell, *The Gauguin Answer Sheet*
Karen Fish, *The Cedar Canoe*
Albert Goldbarth, *Heaven and Earth: A Cosmology*
Pamela Gross, *Birds of the Night Sky/Stars of the Field*
Kathleen Halme, *Every Substance Clothed*
Jonathan Holden, *American Gothic*
Paul Hoover, *Viridian*
Tung-Hui Hu, *The Book of Motion*
Austin Hummell, *The Fugitive Kind*
Claudia Keelan, *The Secularist*
Joanna Klink, *They Are Sleeping*
Maurice Kilwein Guevara, *Postmortem*
Caroline Knox, *To Newfoundland*
Steve Kronen, *Empirical Evidence*

Patrick Lawler, *A Drowning Man Is Never Tall Enough*

Sydney Lea, *No Sign*

Jeanne Lebow, *The Outlaw James Copeland and the Champion-Belted Empress*

Phillis Levin, *Temples and Fields*

Rachel Loden, *Hotel Imperium*

Gary Margolis, *Falling Awake*

Tod Marshall, *Dare Say*

Joshua McKinney, *Saunter*

Mark McMorris, *The Black Reeds*

Mark McMorris, *The Blaze of the Poui*

Laura Mullen, *After I Was Dead*

Jacqueline Osherow, *Conversations with Survivors*

Jacqueline Osherow, *Looking for Angels in New York*

Tracy Philpot, *Incorrect Distances*

Paisley Rekdal, *A Crash of Rhinos*

Donald Revell, *The Gaza of Winter*

Andy Robbins, *The Very Thought of You*

Martha Ronk, *Desire in L.A.*

Martha Ronk, *Eyetrouble*

Tessa Rumsey, *Assembling the Shepherd*

Peter Sacks, *O Wheel*

Aleda Shirley, *Chinese Architecture*

Pamela Stewart, *The Red Window*

Susan Stewart, *The Hive*

Donna Stonecipher, *The Reservoir*

Terese Svoboda, *All Aberration*

Terese Svoboda, *Mere Mortals*

Sam Truitt, *Vertical Elegies 5: The Section*

Lee Upton, *Approximate Darling*

Lee Upton, *Civilian Histories*

Arthur Vogelsang, *Twentieth Century Women*

Sidney Wade, *Empty Sleeves*

Liz Waldner, *Dark Would (The Missing Person)*

Marjorie Welish, *Casting Sequences*

Susan Wheeler, *Bag 'o' Diamonds*

C. D. Wright, *String Light*

Katayoon Zandvakili, *Deer Table Legs*

Andrew Zawacki, *By Reason of Breakings*